John

the man who would be President

by Frederic A. Birmingham
edited by Thomas J. Synhorst

Volume I of the
Presidential Candidate Series

The Curtis Publishing Company   Indianapolis, Indiana

Frederick A. Birmingham and Thomas J. Synhorst
wish to express their gratitude
to the personnel of the following institutions
which assisted with the research:
San Antonio Light, San Antonio, TX
San Antonio Express, San Antonio, TX
U.S. Naval Photographic Center, Washington, D.C.
Wilson County Library, Floresville, TX

JOHN: THE MAN WHO WOULD BE PRESIDENT
Editor/Publisher: Thomas J. Synhorst
Copy Editors: Jenine Howard, Holly G. Miller,
Patrick Perry
Editorial Assistants: Steve Cecil, Kandy K. Kramer
Production: David M. Price
Art Associates: Steven W. Frye, Pam Starkey,
Bill Stemler
Compositors: Penny Allison, Kathy Simpson,
Patricia Stricker, Paula Matlock

CONTENTS

Introduction
Roots

The man of the soil who has never lost touch
with the source of his strength and birthright. Page 1

Statesman

Early politicking at the University of Texas.
Secretary of the U.S. Navy. Secretary of the U.S. Treasury.
An international influence. Three-time Governor of Texas.
Careers in law, business and now politics again. Page 19

Rancher

The place: the Connally Picosa Ranch in Floresville, Texas,
center of Connally clan gatherings, and John's favorite retreat.
Farmer, rancher, sportsman, conservationist, political planner. Page 45

Nellie

Idanell Brill Connally, a quiet presence and
inspirational partner, a great lady for all seasons. Page 67

Campaign

The great American four-year cult celebration of charisma,
character, strategy, strength, oratory, determination, perspiration,
the battlegrounds of votes, cheers, jeers and
$1,000 for a plate of rubberized chicken. Page 79

Issues

A new approach for the politician: talk to the voters about real
issues—and talk straight. Numbered foremost among those real issues:
the Middle East, the Economy, Agriculture and National Security. Page 111

Introduction

In his bedroom closet on his ranch John Connally keeps a sharp ax. Now and then John takes it out and cuts wood with it. If you want to know John Connally you must know about that ax and how he comes to use it so skillfully.

There is a breed of men in America with their roots in the land. They once fed America and earned their existence in the days before tractors and rural electricity. Farm implements were pulled by horses and mules. Water was pumped by hand, from wells dug by hand. Homes were heated and meals were cooked with wood that was cut with axes and hand-pulled cross-cut saws and split with wedges. The trademark of the era was the kerosene lamp; the children studied by it at night. John Connally is one of this breed—raised in that era.

It was a family endeavor; children worked soon after they could walk. Boys worked with men. John Connally walked behind the mules plowing and cultivating back and forth and back again ankle-deep in loose dirt—reins tied behind his back. Twenty miles of plowing a day was common. Then there was haying time, wading waist-deep in hay on hayracks and tromping it away in hot haymows where the temperature sometimes exceeded 120°F. As a boy John pulled those big cotton sacks down the cotton rows. In winter they cut cords of wood for the fire.

Before and after each day's work there were cows and hogs to be fed. Always there were the one or two family cows to milk. A boy would hold the bucket between his knees and squat on a little stool with his head stuck in the steamy side of the cow. Now and then if squeezed too hard, a displeased cow would whip the coarse end strands of her tail, sharply striking the cheek of the hapless milker.

Farm boys in those days were hard and thin, like twisted barbed wire. Throughout the land farm boys lucky enough to go on to college found it difficult to learn to swim; they had so little body fat they sank like rocks.

On the farm in the days of horses, mules and kerosene, no one who could work felt poor or deprived; each was as good as his neighbor. Sweat was sacred, little effort was wasted on foolish sport. Today, one rarely finds one of those with his real roots in the land on the tennis courts or golf links. If he must get some exercise he'll get it back on the farm where it won't be wasted.

Today there are politicians who grew up with electric lights, flush toilets, tennis courts and milk delivered to the door. They talk of the poor as if they were so many birds to feed in the backyard. John Connally was poor when the poor had so much dignity they never used or knew the word. He talks of the dignity and joy in the opportunity to work. To have been a strong, thin boy barefoot behind a mule is a large advantage for a modern politician.

There are lots of ways to describe John Connally. He's a tall Texan, born in the Texas tradition in the shadow of the Alamo. He's loyal to his friends but hard and tough in a fight. He's an over-achiever. Since his college days, men have sought his advice. He's a born leader who always ends up in charge. And he's a winner who has never lost a contest. But don't miss the most important point. John Connally was a poor country boy who learned how to work when he learned how to walk. He comes from those self-reliant people; he's never forgotten.

John Connally is straining for a triple prize, in awesome ascendancy of importance. First, to establish a position during the primaries which will give him clout at the nominating convention. Second, to tread the political high wire during the convention itself, so that his best weapons are not turned against him by some political legerdemain during the infighting common to such bloodlettings. Third, without putting the whammy on himself by thinking about it too much, still to prepare himself for the Presidency, should lightning strike and he find himself on top of the world in November.

The auguries, such as they are, are good for Connally at this point in the race. In the midst of the primaries, he stands well as a contender. According to the public opinion polls, which influence the odds even as they quote them, Ronald Reagan is the front-runner among the Republicans. But that is not entirely an advantage to Mr. Reagan. John B. Connally is a fighter to the core, and the tougher it gets, the better he looks—and the American voter likes a come-from-behind competitor in any kind of horse race. The other worthy candidates, Howard Baker, Robert Dole, George Bush and Philip Crane, are campaigning briskly and bravely, but you can't help thinking that their only hope is to hang on and hope for a Reagan/Connally deadlock at the convention and a win in the dark horse role.

And, so far, Big John is showing a lot of early foot in the race. He's making friends and he's making headlines. And the offstage gossip is that front-runner Reagan is making the same speech too many times, is forgetting a lot of names he should remember (Connally's memory for names and faces is phenomenal) and there's also that nagging whisper that Reagan would finish his first term of office at age 72, not necessarily, but possibly, too old for another term.

Connally's headlines are in the right spots. For instance, in a recent issue of *The New York Times Magazine*, the editor of *The American Lawyer* magazine, Steven Brill, wrote an article

headlined: "Connally: Coming On Tough ... As the 1980 Presidential campaign heats up, the former Governor of Texas hopes to tough-talk his way into the White House."

Author Brill, in an extensive critique which dips deep into Connally's political past and questions some of his turn-around statements and actions, nevertheless starts out in a manner which suggests that he, too, has fallen victim to the famous Connally charm and straight-from-the-shoulder talk. In the article's opening words:

At 6 o'clock on a fall evening in New York, John B. Connally strides into a cocktail reception at the Board Room, a Park Avenue businessmen's club. He looks taller than he is, his 6-foot 2-inch frame enlarged by perfectly tailored suits and a magnetic self-confidence. All eyes turn to him.

The men in the Board Room, each of whom had paid or pledged $1,000 to the Connally Presidential campaign, are not accustomed to playing supporting roles: John Loeb, of Shearson Loeb Rhoades; John deButts, former chairman of A.T.&T.; William Spencer, president of Citibank; John Whitehead of Goldman Sachs; I.W. Burnham of Drexel Burnham Lambert; Robert Belfer of Belfer Petroleum; William Ward Foshay, the managing partner of the Wall Street firm of Sullivan & Cromwell.

John Connally, the 62-year-old former Secretary of the Treasury and Governor of Texas, moves easily among them, breezily patting backs and acknowledging support, the businessman's rock star surrounded by his groupies.

On the first page of the same article:

"I guess I'll vote for him," a Fort Worth cab driver who voted for John Kennedy, Lyndon Johnson, Richard Nixon and Jimmy Carter said a week before Connally's New York trip. ... "He's smart and he won't take any bull from anybody. We've been so worried what people around the world think of us, or about pleasing minorities or some ethics teacher in some college somewhere that we're going under. He'll stop that."

Connally can hardly be unaware of the admiring comment about him. Richard Morehead said in the *Dallas Morning News* that "Connally fits just as easily into a Governor's chair, an oilman's office, a cowman's saddle or a drawing room as men who were born to those stations." The political editor of the *Houston Post*, William H. Gardner, described Connally in 1969 as "urbane, polished and handsome. People used to say: He looks like a Governor ought to look. He was the friend of one President and shot down at the side of another, a traveler to foreign lands, an inspiring political leader, a national figure, a man used to high levels and inner circles."

He was dubbed "an individualist, and a leader of whatever ship he's on."

But the most extravagant praise was heaped on John Connally by a veteran newspaperman, often a vitriolic critic of the Washington crowd, James J. Kilpatrick, who announced "the explosive emergence of John B. Connally" as Secretary of the Treasury when President Nixon put him in that Cabinet role with the words: "Connally comes on like West Texas sunshine."

What's more, purred Kilpatrick:

John Connally seems to have something special.

Part of his appeal doubtless arises from the contrast he brings to his drab surroundings. The Nixon Administration has its merits, but pizzazz it has not.

Now comes Connally, six-feet-two, silver man, with a handsome face and a he-man tan. He stands straight as the shaft of a six-iron. In private conversation he looks you straight in the eye, but it is not like it was with Lyndon. Mr. Johnson had the flinty eye of a faro dealer. Connally has the friendly gaze of a good coach or a parish priest. Want to buy a used car? This guy could sell an old Toyota to Henry Ford.

. . . here in Credibility Gulch, he possesses one attribute more precious than nuggets of gold— the appearance of absolute candor. . . . Connally, at 54, has the look of eagles; and he is flying high to somewhere.

As a mere journalist, not an analyst, happily, I have no political reputation or savvy to risk. On this firm basis of avowed ignorance, I eschew all caution and predict that John Connally will win out in all three phases of his coming run for the Presidency, and will win it all in the end.

The candidate himself, never a man lacking in confidence, apparently agrees. He has never run for an office that he didn't expect to win, and he has never lost.

This was reflected in a conversation I enjoyed with John's vivacious and attractive wife, Idanell ("Nellie") Connally on the day after Thanksgiving during a family gathering at the Connallys' 9,000-acre showplace Picosa Ranch, near Floresville in southeast Texas. Although Nellie habitually keeps a low profile on matters political and has always done so during her husband's varied career, it is known that Nellie and John talk things over at length privately. They think alike on important matters.

So her response to a possibly impertinent question of mine is still quite indicative of how John feels about the same thing.

I tried to phrase The Big Question to the lady as gently as possible.

"If the Governor is nominated, and if he goes on to be elected, how do you think you will enjoy the view from Harry Truman's White House balcony porch?"

Nellie just flashed a smile and then corrected me gently.

"You mean . . . *when* John wins the nomination and *when* he is elected President, don't you?" she teased.

But she meant it.

John expects to win.

The hazards still ahead of him are horrific, not the least of which is the gravest hazard each candidate must face and overcome—himself. Political history is alive with tiny slips of the tongue which blew the campaign wide open and obliterated the candidate.

Although he did not actually utter the phrase, Republican James G. Blaine never bothered to repudiate the words he was supposed to have applied in 1884 to his opponents as the party of "rum, Romanism and rebellion." It blew him right out of the water with the voters.

That's the classic historical goof of a Presidential campaign lost by loose words. But I have a more recent and equally telling incident which arose during a friendly dinner with a famous New York attorney. It was well that he was the host, because we were ensconced in one of those posh Manhattan restaurants where the menu is so elegant that the prices of the selections are discreetly omitted. One merely signs the check later without deigning to care what it totals.

This took place shortly after the 1948 election in which Harry Truman's electrifying "Garrison Finish" against Republican Thomas E. Dewey took everyone by such surprise (except for Harry himself, who never lacked for fighting spirit, either) that *The Chicago Tribune* even ran a headline announcing "Dewey Defeats Truman," a blooper Harry gleefully displayed for the rest of his life whenever the opportunity was offered.

At any rate, my friend and I were seated in this hushed restaurant next to the very table where the vanquished was dining alone in gloomy solitude.

"The gentleman at the table next to us," said my companion *sotto voce*, "is the most disappointed man in America this evening. Yet he has only himself to blame. The truth is that during the campaign he contrived to wear the mantle of the Presidency with such success that when Election Day came around, the voters decided that it was time for a change."

John Connally is not about to make the same mistake, or any other mistake of this fatal nature, I trust. He is too canny a campaigner for that. He has studied the opposition both in his own and in the Democratic Party and he is sincerely convinced—and he looks you right in the eye when he says so—that he is the most qualified man to sit in the Oval Office.

I am looking at John Connally as one concerned American who measures a man who has a fighting chance to be our Chief Executive. This is not going to be an ordinary election by past standards. There have been contests settled by pure personal charisma in previous elections. If so, John would win this one hands down, despite the Kennedy smile and accent. Connally makes heads turn, even in places where they do not know his name or who he is. He's that kind of man. In this election, it may not be inaccurate to say that character, after all, is going to be the main issue.

Give or take a few phrases, all of the candidates face the same major problems: Contain Russia. Defuse the Middle East. Find workable domestic policies for inflation, energy, social structuring and government effectiveness. It is possible that the candidate who convinces the electorate that he has the leadership to restore America's posture in the world and rekindle confidence in effective administration at home will be the one who wins, regardless of the so-called issues.

It could be Connally. So, he merits a closer look. Not that he is an easy man to know. Quite the opposite.

There is a wide spectrum of opinion on J.B.C. He has been glorified and vilified by experts (his reaction to both is about the same). For instance, one very informed and businesslike newspaperwoman and columnist in John's own native Wilson County allows her sharply pointed pencil to dangle loosely in her fingers and stars to spangle her eyes as she voices the theory that over every sizable span of years this nation seems to breed a giant to come forth and save its soul just when it needs it most. She cites George Washington, then Abe Lincoln, and in her view John B. Connally is today's man of destiny come forth to solve our crisis of spirit and purpose.

Her dedication should not be taken lightly.

Three others agree with her to the extent of saying that John B. Connally is the man who should someday be our President. That opinion was voiced at various times by Lyndon B. Johnson, Richard Nixon and Gerald Ford, all of whom should know something about the office.

On the other hand, Connally has his critics and some of them are scathing. Yet at times there creeps into the vitriol a few drops of grudging admiration. Says one, filled with hate and reluctant recognition: "John is meaner than an alligator with abscessed teeth, but he's also a hell of an interesting animal to watch."

It doesn't all come down to the fact that he's a Texan, but there's a lot of Texas in John. It takes a lifetime to even try to understand Texas, if only its size. As they say, "Was a time they thought of dividing it up a bit, and it turned out that they'd have room enough to make five states out of Texas—but they couldn't decide who'd get the Alamo!"

These days John Connally, former Governor, Cabinet officer, Navy Secretary and world traveler, dresses like a conservative businessman and statesman, both of which he is, and wears the style with distinction on Wall Street, in Washington, D.C., and in his Houston law offices. Relaxing in ranch clothes down in Floresville, Texas, he can look just like one of the boys.

All the same, he's got Texas in him, and to my thinking, that's good. The renowned George Sessions Perry once remarked: "I have said how much horse sense the ordinary Texan has. If you're all right, Texans divine it and accept you, and unless you aren't accepted, you'll never know how much that means. If you're not quite on the level, you'll just tread water in Texas and never be standing on solid ground—and money won't make the difference."

So now let's have a look at a Texan in the limelight today. John B. Connally, the man who would be the President of the United States. ★

Frederic A. Birmingham

Roots

*"There are only two lasting bequests we can
hope to give our children. One of these is
roots...the other, wings."*
—John B. Connally, quoting from
Henry Ward Beecher

John B. Connally has roots deep in the rich,
sandy loam of the upper coastal plains of south
central Texas.

He was born February 27, 1917, in Floresville, Texas, a bare hundred miles from the
southern coast which sends Gulf breezes in summer across the rolling range and keeps the win-
ters mild. There's still plenty of mesquite and
cactus to tear at a horseman's chaps, and once
upon a time hackberry and scrub oak possessed
the land, but today all that has been cleared. The
best of the live oaks have been spared and stand
like sentinels on the hills or clustered around the
farms and ranch houses. The loam is underlaid
by black soil for one or two feet, providing
drought-resisting qualities. Today peanuts are
a million-dollar crop in Wilson County. The
farmland is rich in pecan trees, and water-
melons, black-eyed peas, corn and peach trees
spring from the soil. The grazing fields are dot-
ted with milk and beef cattle. It is open country.
Horizons stretch into an eternity here. The
sky—since this is Texas—seems to be bigger and
higher than anywhere else.

This is storied land. When the Spanish con-
quistadors rode in to the jingle of silver spurs in
the 18th century, the native Comanche,
Tonkawa and Lipan-Apache tribes fought them
tooth and nail for the domain. Yet, drenched in
gore, it became part of the Spanish frontier.
Governor Martin de Alarcon founded San Antonio in 1718 (it was then called Villa de Bexar).
In 1830, Francisco Flores de Abreyo founded the
first hacienda in the area. Floresville, named
after him, still is home to his descendants.

Texas became a state in 1836, March 2, on the
birthday of Sam Houston. There were the car-
petbag years after 1865. There were range wars
after that, enough to make a hundred Hollywood
horse operas, as the open-range ranchers cut the
barbed wire of the homesteaders, and gunplay
exploded a-plenty. But by 1884, the Wilson County courthouse, seen on the page opposite, was
built as a seat of law and order, and the noble
figure of blind justice, battered ever since by
winds and rains, finally stood atop the façade, as
she still does today.

When you think of John Connally's heritage,
never forget this. Down the pike just a few miles
from Floresville in San Antonio stands the
sacred symbol of all Texans—the Alamo. There,
although given the chance to escape, Davy
Crockett and Jim Bowie and that tiny group of
proud and fierce Texans elected to stay and fight
to the death against the overwhelming odds of
the Mexican army in the struggle for
Lone Star independence.

The spirit of the Alamo is the birthright of
every Texas boy and girl.

Born in the shadow of that hallowed place, be
sure of it, the boy John was a fighter from the
very day of his birth. ★

On January 27, 1908, John Bowden Connally, Sr., born April 18, 1889, married Lela Wright from Fairview, a community near Floresville —the two of 'em sitting bolt upright, sweet and sassy, in a horse-n-buggy. Lela was from a family of nine children, all of whom picked cotton as a means of income after their father's death. A thoughtful and intelligent girl, she taught in a country school. Her personal rule for success in life: education and hard work. Six-foot-five John Sr. had two generations of Texas Connallys behind him, all rugged and God-fearing men, descendants of the immigration of the first Connallys from Ireland during the great potato famine of the 19th century. (One of them, our present John's grandfather, John Wesley Connally, carried the same name as the former Texas gunslinger, John Wesley Hardin, because their fathers were good friends and both admired the great Methodist churchman, John Wesley.)

There were eight Connally children to come: Wyatt (1900), who died as a child in a tragic household accident when he strayed too close to an open fire, an all-too-frequent frontier hazard; Stanford (1911); Carmen (1914); John (1917); Golfrey (1919); Merrill (1921); Wayne (1923); Blanche (1925).

John Jr. learned about work and determination from his father, who tried practically everything to make a living. "The Depression never touched us," says John today. "We were so far down economically, we hardly knew it happened." His father was, in turn, a bricklayer, barber college student, tenant farmer, butcher, operator of a bus line and, finally, a landowner in Floresville.

John's early boyhood was spent working on the farm his father rented. He learned to do all those things which made the farmers so self-reliant and capable. He dragged his share of cotton sacks. He harnessed the mules and spent long days behind them as they pulled the plows, harrow disks and cultivators. He never forgot the feel of fresh-plowed dirt beneath bare feet. Even after the family moved to town, John worked on the farm in summers to make spending money. ★

2

John worked away from the farm as well,
delivering milk and performing chores for the
townspeople who still remember his clothes
patched at elbows, knees and other strategic spots
to hold things together. He found time, thanks to
his parents' encouragement, to work hard as well
at his studies at Floresville High School (right).

Churchgoing was an important part of young
John's upbringing, giving him moral and spiritual
values and his first touch of social life, since the
Connally kids all worked too hard to have time for
extracurricular activities at school. The First
Methodist Church in Floresville (above) had a
busy Sunday school, and the Epworth League,
where all of the Connally children were appointed
speakers for the meetings, met on Sunday evening.
Here, John got his first taste for oratory. ★

Attendance at church was a law in the Connally family, Lela saw to that, unless there was some dire emergency which would take precedence for family survival. Hard work, sobriety and other Christian virtues were part of the Connally upbringing. Neither beer nor whiskey ever was drunk in the family household, and even dancing was not encouraged. But, since John escorted his sister to parties on the insistence of his dad, who was old-fashioned enough to believe a girl should have protection, John managed to learn how things go at community get-togethers. ★

There are plenty of tales around Floresville of the mischief the Connally boys could get into. True, they were high-spirited kids who had all the usual scraps and scufflings even among themselves. But in general, their reputation was good, probably influenced by the strict discipline imposed by the parents. The father was too big a man physically to punish his children, but Lela was never one to spare the rod. John's sister Carmen has a revealing memory today when she smilingly recalls: "People used to say there were never any branches on the peach trees over at the Connally place. They'd all been used for switches."

And she adds: "John got his share."

John Jr., something of a fatalist, says he would change only one thing in his life if he could. "I would have hoped my father could have lived longer." (John Connally, Sr., died in 1950 at the age of 62.) "He was the most important influence on my life. He was smart, determined, independent and proud."

The boy John grew up fast. He knew what he wanted out of life. One Christmas, he asked for a gun, a rope and a Bible. As for a career, he wanted to be a cowboy, or a lawyer or a preacher—he ultimately became the first two, and, as Governor of Texas, highly relished an opportunity to make a pass at playing preacher when he dedicated a new church in Bandera, where his sister lived. John learned a bit about "favorite sons" when, as a poor kid, he lost a debating contest he had clearly won, in favor of the son of a prominent local family from the "right side of the tracks." Undaunted, he came back and won the district Texas Interscholastic League championship in declamation. He could sense something of future potential from that. From the fifth grade on he was an outstanding speaker, specializing in Joaquin Miller's "The Defense of The Alamo" and making the rafters ring with Patrick Henry's "I know not what course others may take; but as for me, give me liberty or give me death."

Then, as now, Floresville had a large Mexican population. John learned early to mix Spanish and English in the easy give-and-take on Main Street. ★

Both John's mother and his dad wanted a college education for him. With some sacrifice, they were able to start him out at the University of Texas at the tender age of 16. He was big and good-looking ... a farmboy type who liked other people so much he found it easy to overcome shyness.

John took the university campus by storm. This was just the place for leadership and political action, and his latent abilities in both quickly surfaced. On the side, he took a great interest in dramatics and, as a member of the campus Curtain Club, performed many plays, among them *Marco Millions* and *Liliom*. In the latter he played the part of the "richly dressed man," which suited young John to a T. In a scene from one of the Curtain Club plays (right) the young actors (John, center) have allowed themselves to be upstaged by an antique sofa.

John's extracurricular accomplishments at the university were stupendous. There were those in that huge student body who later went on to bigger things, but John was the pick of the lot. ★

6

Before he was through he was elected president of the student body, dean of his legal fraternity and president of his law class. It was said that by the time he ran for president of the student body in 1937, John knew 60 percent of the 100,000-member student body on a first- or last-name basis. He was president of the Curtain Club for three years and chairman of the board of student publications, which directed the *Daily Texan* newspaper, a monthly magazine, and the yearbook, the *Cactus*. He was chairman of the board of the student union; president of the prestigious Athenaeum Literary Society and president of the Wesley Players. He was winner of the 1934 intersociety oratorical contest, a member of the Curtain Club board of directors, vice-president of the 1935 freshman law class, a member of Delta Theta Phi legal fraternity and a member of the Hildebrand Society. In 1938, he was president of the Student Assembly, which paid a $30-a-month salary. This he relished, since he was supplementing money from home by selling mints and gum in the dormitories. On the opposite page is a picture of the Assembly. No trouble finding big John: front row center. ★

John met the love of his life at the university. She was Idanell Brill of Austin, a self-professed "frustrated thespian" who joined the Curtain Club and became its secretary while he was president. John had been cutting a wide swath among the co-eds, but the perky little brunette freshman swept the Big-Man-On-Campus junior off his feet. Demure "Nellie," not unaware of John's dashing looks and "vested interests" (note membership keys proudly displayed in photo), once revealed to him that the night she met him was the high point of her university years. ★

A fine arts major, Nellie had the same knack as John in winning honor in her own way. She was chosen a "Bluebonnet Belle," one of the Ten Most Beautiful during her freshman year, queen of the Texas Relays during her sophomore year and "Sweetheart of the University" in her junior year. At the Curtain Club's annual banquet in 1938, John won awards for the best interpretation of character and use of his voice, but Nellie made off also with a prize for best interpretation of character and the best sense of timing. Perhaps now we can smile a bit at the seriousness of such campus triumphs, after the years pass. But, still, they are the stuff of youth and dreams and neither is to be taken lightly. One thing is for sure, Nellie's timing *was* perfect: She and John were married December 21, 1940. ★

In 1941, when World War II struck, John was engaged in the private practice of law, but, as a member of the naval reserve, he was off to active duty in the U.S. Navy in December, 1941. He was to serve all the way through. Even as a reserve Navy ensign, which is the way he started his active duty, John Connally seemed to be where important things were happening. He spent six months with Dr. Barker of Columbia University, setting up a war training program. It was designed to teach civilian shipyard workers in Navy shipyards and in private ones like the Kaiser yard how to mass-produce ships. He worked for Under Secretary of the Navy James Forrestal.

When General Eisenhower was planning his campaign through North Africa, Sicily and Italy, the State Department assigned an experienced ambassador to handle the touchy international affairs as armed troops crossed and recrossed national borders. The man was Robert Murphy. With him, to North Africa, he took a talented staff of young officers—one of them was John Connally. ★

John Connally came back in the fall of 1943 on a B-24 with, among others, Elliot Roosevelt. It was one of those "hairy" trips. The plane's navigational equipment and radio aids failed. They were lost most of the night. They came down 900 miles off course in St. John's, Newfoundland, instead of Goosebay, Labrador.

John was always pushing for combat duty, and finally he made it. First in the radar room of the *Franklini*, then, in 1945 as combat information center officer and night combat air controller aboard the aircraft carriers *Essex* and *Bennington*. The *Essex*, flagship for a carrier group operating off the Japanese Coast, was battered by three typhoons and attacked by kamikaze fighter planes, but rode them all out. John was awarded the Legion of Merit, combat ribbons with nine battle stars and the Bronze Star for valor in action. ★

As the war in the Pacific began to tilt in favor of the U.S. forces and our fleet smashed its way nearer and nearer to the homeland of Japan, suddenly a new and fanatic weapon was turned against the American ships. Dauntless Japanese flyers prayed to their ancestors and, with planes loaded to the hilt with bombs, took off for suicide flights against the enemy. Their tactic was simply to use their pilot controls so as to serve as guided missiles—their mission was to fly straight at the target, a U.S. ship, and crash-land to certain destruction in order to wreak maximum havoc. ★

It was an offensive kind of madness against which no defense had been drawn up, yet the accuracy of U.S. gunfire for the most part was equal to this tactic of ultimate desperation. Among the ships struck by kamikaze suicide attacks was the *U.S.S. Essex*, the carrier on which John Connally served. These remarkable Navy photographs show the ship smoking and wounded from the onslaught in the seas off Okinawa. Thanks to accurate anti-aircraft fire, the attacking planes—most, but not all—were shot out of the air. ★

After being mustered out of the Navy in 1946, John Connally decided to exercise another youthful bent he had touched upon. He had been a disc jockey and regular announcer on the campus radio at the University of Texas (when in the world did he find time for that?) and he had once worked in Austin for Lyndon Johnson's station there, KTBC. Now, John and a group of Service buddies organized a new radio station in Austin, aptly named KVET; the one in the middle is their president and manager. Name: John B. Connally. He borrowed $25,000 to gain this august position, and his monthly fee on this eminence was in the neighborhood of $250. ★

John has a yen for music (he enjoys everything from the classics to popular, and has a special fondness for the records of the great Swedish tenor, Jussi Bjoerling) that started a long time ago. Way back in the early days of the Epworth League at the First Methodist Church in Floresville, the Connally kids often played instrumental trios for League socials—Carmen on the trombone, Golfrey on the violin, and John on the saxophone. In his high school years, he tooted his saxophone in the school band. The photo at left, taken years later in a moment of adult reminiscence, suggests that John's private opinion of his musical skills may have been a deciding motivation for his career in politics. Above, John handles the broadcasting of news, sports and music with obvious verve at KVET, from 6 a.m. to midnight on the 1,000-watt station. It is still going strong under the management of one of the original stockholders. ★

John's mother Lela is now 90 and lives in a rest home in Bandera, Texas, which is owned by John's sister Carmen and her husband Speedy Hicks. Lela is known for her wit, and when she talks, her eyebrows go up and down just like John's. People say that John has inherited his father's determination and his mother's sense of humor. They say John looks more like his mother than his father, especially around the eyes. Lela and John Sr. thought alike—they both believed that no work was too hard to do and that it was never too early to get up and start at it. They both believed that a man can make out of his life whatever he has a mind to. ★

John Connally retains tender memories of the old homestead at Floresville, Texas (upper left), where he learned about hard work and the ethics of a useful life. Those early memories go back still another generation as John (lower left) visits the grave of Grandfather Haddox. To relive the happy Floresville days, John and the other "Connally kids" gather (below) with mother Lela, who perhaps remembers that spirited time of family life best. ★

ronald
anderson

Statesman

The original painting from which the photograph on the opposite page was made hangs in the big family room at the Picosa Ranch. Obviously it is a composite of the life of John Connally—farm boy, campus careerist, naval officer, lawyer, rancher, Secretary of the Navy and of the U.S. Treasury, three-time Governor of the state of Texas—with appropriate decorative symbols of power and place.

Behind the visuals is a life of astonishing virtuosity. It has been said—after reflecting that John Connally has known four U.S. Presidents on a personal and official basis: Eisenhower, Kennedy, Johnson and Nixon—that he might have good reason to consider himself a candidate better qualified than any of them at a similar career point. As Texas' 38th Governor, Connally ran an enormous business called state government—he had a budget of $3 billion and more than 200,000 employees. His experience was not parochial, either. He learned a national stance as early as his first years in Washington, as secretary to Representative Lyndon B. Johnson of Texas. Early on in his career, even during World War II, he had world assignments which brought him into contact with such figures as James Forrestal, Ike Eisenhower and Edward Stettinius. As Secretary of the Navy and later the Treasury, obviously, he became a participant in the international scene. He was a member of the President's Foreign Intelligence Advisory Board in '70 and '71, and was reappointed to that office by Presidents Nixon and Ford, serving up through '74. On one mission or another he worked with top figures in India, the Middle East, and South America, and met with people like Indira Gandhi, Argentine President Alejandro Lanusse and the calculating sheiks of Saudi Arabia. He was envied and sometimes hated for the personal rapport he enjoyed at the White House with Johnson, Nixon and Ford, each one of whom publicly stated at one time or another that Connally was of Presidential timbre. Sam Rayburn, the powerful Speaker of the House, said of John when he was being considered by Kennedy in '61 as Secretary of the Navy, "Connally is one of the ablest men of his age I have known. I think he is capable of doing a fine job in any position in which he is placed."

It was good training for a man who would be President. ★

John was a bang-up Secretary of the Navy. It didn't hurt with the high-ranking brass, who had groaned under several Secretaries who couldn't handle a rowboat and thought that the "port" side had something to do with wine, that *this* Secretary of the Navy had been to sea and seen plenty of combat duty in World War II. "I see no substitute for sea power," said the Navy's new boss. "Our most probable call to battle will be that resulting from the nibbling, tantalizing tactics of potential enemies . . . and here—as we have for years—the Navy-Marine air-sea-ground teams excel." He could have been talking about one of our pressing needs for the '80s.

Speaking to his officers about what they might say in public: "Recognize and accept your own responsibility by insisting on being quoted by name, rank and billet. . . . In short, if you are not willing to be quoted by name, you should not be speaking."

Connally was often out with the fleet, where he was much more popular than with certain admirals in the Pentagon, who had to navigate under forced draft and set their alarm clocks for action as big John piped them aboard for 7 a.m. sessions. ★

John Connally took his career seriously in small jobs, too. We see, opposite, a Seascout getting the thrill of a lifetime with a handshake from Number One.

There was another Navy man in John's life, and that was President John F. Kennedy, himself a much-decorated war hero. The two men had a lot in common: Both were fighting types, packed with vigor and vitality, with a tremendous zest for the acquisition and use of sheer power and a faculty for enjoying the rough and tumble—and bare knuckles, when necessary—of the political life. Neither one had a taste for playing second fiddle. Both worked hard and had a talent for making the machinery work to back up an ideal. Other than that, they were very dissimilar—the rich boy from Massachusetts, Ivy League all the way, and the dirt-poor Texan, University of Texas and all that. Their political outlooks were, not unsurprisingly, quite often at opposite poles. Under the skin, though, they were the same breed, tough and uncompromising politicians who recognized in each other a matching charisma and clout. Kennedy saw Connally as a potential future Presidential opponent. He knew that of the two, Connally might be a bit more popular there. JFK decided that he could benefit from a visit to Dallas as the guest of the state and the Governor. There was vote-getting to be done for the Presidential campaign which Kennedy was eyeing. So he made the fateful decision to go to Texas. ★

No one, least of all John, ever underestimated what his family, and especially his lovely wife Nellie, meant to him as a public figure. They grew along with him and went to Washington and the Governor's mansion with him, and his propensity for having his family around him at all times closed gaps between him and the public which could have been accomplished in no other way. On one occasion, when he had to labor rather more than what he was accustomed to draw applause from a public recital of accomplishments as Governor of Texas, it was noted that what drew the most hand clapping of all was a casual mention, intended almost as a throwaway, that Nellie had illuminated and beautified the grounds of the Governor's mansion in Austin. ★

His parents, especially his mother, had always stressed the importance of education in John's life, and he carried that conviction over to his political priorities. It was not difficult for him, therefore, to heft a flask of mercury at the dedication of a new science facility at the junior college in Corpus Christi. His interest and gratification were not in the least feigned. The same thing happens when John gets on a horse for a parade—you can't fool a Texan when it comes to riding, and this guy clearly comes off as having been there before. ★

On November 22, 1963, John applauded President and Mrs. Kennedy as they prepared to ride in a motorcade through the streets of Dallas. For J.F.K., death waited along the route. He and Jackie and Nellie were all smiles, but John, as he is seated in the open car, looks concerned in the picture (opposite). Nellie Connally is convinced that a separate bullet—not the one which struck the President, as some maintained—hit Connally, smashing through his back and chest, collapsing his right lung and emerging to fracture his right wrist. The bullet also creased his right thigh. As the assassin fired, John turned slightly, hearing the noise, and only that seemed to have kept the bullet from going right through his heart. ★

Nellie and Jackie kept their vigil of horror as surgeons worked frantically over the two shattered victims at the hospital. We know the rest. Only John Connally survived. Nellie wrote in a magazine article, "I do not know why the President had to die—that vital and hard-working young man—or why John was spared. Some things are beyond us; some things we must learn to live with." ★

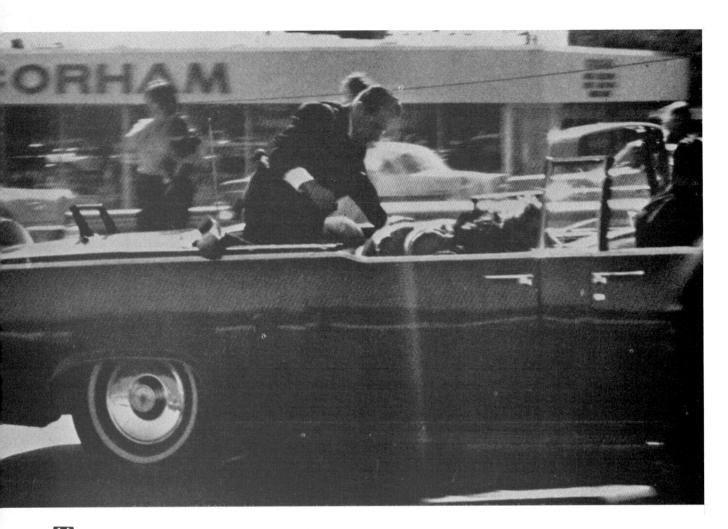

The Kennedy tragedy and his own close shave
with death were to mark John for the rest of his
life; never was he to forget those terrible moments in the car when Camelot was blasted
loose from its moorings. But it had one curious
by-product—it turned a national spotlight on
Connally, and a certain amount of the charisma
and glamorous aura of the young J.F.K. rubbed
off on him. Among the thousands of letters he
received from everywhere, one particularly stood
out. A lady wrote: "It is not up to us to question
God, but He surely held you in the palm of His
hand that day. You must be destined for something wonderful." John had lost one rib in the
operation and, as son Mark described the
damage, the bullet blew a hole in his right chest
the size of a baseball as it exited from his body. ★

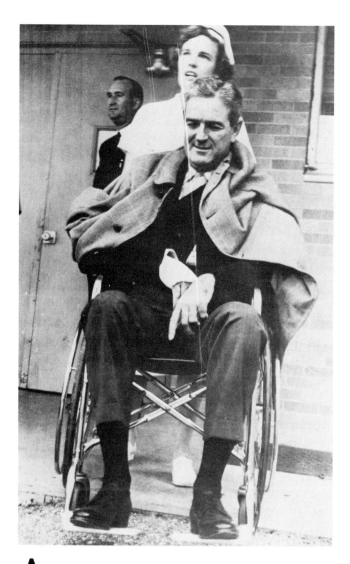

Below, we see Nellie greeting her son Mark as John comes home with her. His hands were still badly damaged where the bullets had hit after plowing through the rest of him. It was some time before John could even shake hands with anyone without wincing; the hand is still a bit stiff for him to use today, on occasion. But what the experience has done to him spiritually was sealed forever in his mind. The assassination as a historical watershed, falling away into the killing of Robert Kennedy and Martin Luther King in the same short span of years, was an emotional turning point from which the nation was never to completely recover. John was one who noticed what this had done to the public conscience and the changing attitude of the time. "We find substantial evidence of the moral erosion in society which should be a danger signal to all of us."

Above, is John shown in a wheelchair during his period of recuperation which took 13 days in the hospital. John's release from Parkland Hospital in Dallas was a time of great family rejoicing and a day marked with excitement, for that matter, all over Texas and beyond.★

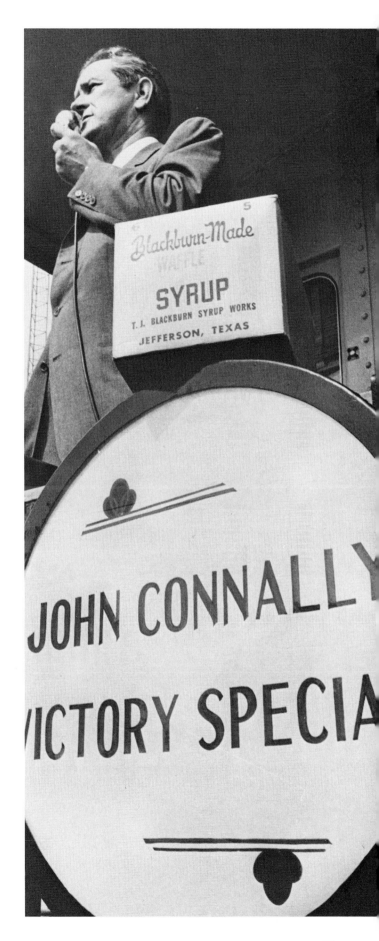

In the days following the assassination of J.F.K., John and Nellie made a tour of Mexico and visited the Governors of all the northern states as part of his Good Neighbor policy between Texas and the nation south of the border. Recalling the days of his youth, swapping tales with the Latins and the Canary Islander descendants of Floresville, John walked through the Mexican streets chatting with the people in Spanish. They really went for him in a big way, so much so that a band was brought all the way from Tampico in Ciudad Victoria to play luncheon music for the Connallys simply because it included in its repertoire that rousing and evoking tune: "The Eyes of Texas Are Upon You."

John turned back to the serious business of politicking with a new sense of purpose. He had always been a good hand at mingling with the so-called "man in the street." Now a closer bond was knitted as people he met in all walks of life recognized the traumatic experience he had survived. They relived in their own hearts how it must have been to sit next to a President of the United States as he was publicly slapped down. There have been many high officials who attempted to show interest in the ordinary man, but it just didn't always come off in every case. Not so with John. Just as he had proved to the men in the Navy that he was one of them as Secretary, John is successful in shooting the breeze with civilians at work. He knows the lingo, and he is familiar with what it is like to work with his hands. He doesn't have to fake it, and this comes through every time. He's a Stetson who is equally comfortable as a hard hat. ★

Every Texan is something of a politician, from the moment he cuts his eyeteeth. Texas has had its politicians in the past who knew all about how to survive in the rough-and-tumble sport of politics, but probably John has been more successful at it and, to tell the truth, has gotten more fun out of it than anyone in the Lone Star State's history. He broke all records in '64, when 1.88 million votes were cast for him in the general election. This contrasted significantly with the 1.66 million votes Texans gave another native of their state, Lyndon B. Johnson, who headed the Democratic ticket. An overwhelming majority of Texans is in accord with John's views and he delights in that response; he can afford to beam as he celebrates an inauguration and receives the arch of swords with his charming wife Nellie. And Nellie and his mother, Lela, can smile, too, at being with such a popular figure in the public eye. Kids may not know much about politics, but they are quick to size up the kind of guy they think they can get along with, and John is their man every time.★

Every busy executive needs an occasional respite from affairs of state, and JBC is no exception. Here, he issues a special proclamation with a little help from a friend (and non-voting constituent). At right, he and Nellie split a wish at the end of a Texas pitch-in barbecue. ★

John is a more thoughtful man than is generally recognized—in that respect his good looks, easy manner and extrovert personality are in the nature of a handicap. "In this changing world," he has said, "our most important resource is the mind of man," and he means it. He overhauled the educational system in Texas to the extent that at one point he had quadrupled the number of technical courses taught in the state's junior colleges.

"All this country needs," a Texan in the 1860s was supposed to have observed, "is more water and a few nice people."

"Man," the story has General Philip Sheridan saying, "that is all *hell* needs."

John Connally spent a lot of time as Governor developing Texas resources, protecting wilderness areas, expanding parks and recreational facilities and—to quote a report on the subject—"That which is God-given to Texas has been retooled, updated and extended" under Governor Connally. ★

World traveler and good will ambassador, John Connally is a quick study. Be it photography, cattle breeding or ecology and African jungle life, Connally quickly grasps the essentials and is soon contributing to the field. Above, Connally photographs some Afrikander cattle at the State Fair in Salisbury, Rhodesia. From behind they bear a striking resemblance to his Santa Gertrudis breed. Rhodesian Santa Gertrudis were being shown nearby. ★

John Connally visited Africa in the summer of 1978. While there he flew to Salisbury, where he met with then-Premier Ian Smith and three moderate black leaders fighting the Soviet and Chinese-backed terrorists. Here he is pictured with the Reverend Sithole, a moderate Rhodesian nationalist. The new name for Rhodesia will be Zimbabwe, the ruins and famous civilization once living in ancient Rhodesia. The name means as much to black Zimbabweans as the Alamo means to Texans. ★

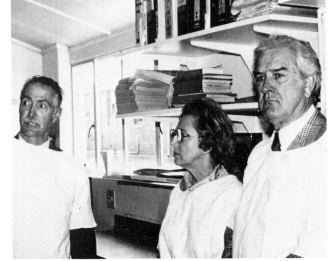

Mrs. Claire Chennault, whose husband commanded the Flying Tigers of World War II fame, is a close friend of "former naval person" John Connally. They have both worked for a stronger U.S. fleet in the Pacific to counter growing Soviet naval might in the Far East. ★

South Africa's black population is among the fastest growing in the world thanks to free medical care and excellent hospitals (opposite center). John and Nellie Connally are given a tour of *Baragwanagh*, the largest hospital in the southern hemisphere.

The hospital includes a large fertility clinic which helps black women who wish to become pregnant.

Above, John visits with Mrs. Ethel Thebehali, wife of the popular mayor of Soweto, David Thebehali. Mrs. Thebehali is a registered nurse. The Thebehalis are moderates, are not bitter toward whites and advocate long-term peace and cooperation between the races. Connally was popular everywhere in Africa among all races, as well as with farmers, businessmen, government leaders and the "man on the street."★

Rancher

Of all the moments in his rewarding life, John Connally is perhaps the happiest when he sits behind the desk upstairs at his retreat, the 9,000-acre Picosa Ranch, just off the balcony and well out of earshot of the TV and conversations going on under the cathedral ceiling in the two-storied living room/den below.

He sits behind the massive 6-foot oak desk he occupied in his three terms as Governor of Texas. In front of the desk stretches out a huge rug made of the skin of a Tasmanian lion. On the walls are photographs of the great, but none is larger than that of an obviously enlarged, framed picture of an elderly man in shirt sleeves. Connally glances at it thoughtfully: "My father."

There is a picture window overlooking his land, stretching as far as the eye can see. Near it is a standing rack of Winchester rifles, expensive beauties that have the look of readiness for immediate action. There are no gates at the entrance to the ranch, a half mile or so off the "main" road (called the "Independence Trail": A brawny arm brandishing a rifle is the symbol of the Trail sign), but as you enter, a Rhodesian Ridgeback dog and a passel of other guardians yip out and escort your car all the way to the main house, speculating among themselves on the probable succulence of a bite or two. The road is rough, I suspect, because the Governor does not hanker after casual sightseers. He could have Secret Service protection these days if he wanted it, but he prefers not to burden the taxpayers with the cost. I have a hunch he figures his Winchesters might serve just as well. John is a crack shot, and only a few steps from his front door is a skeet-shooting range if his trigger finger gets itchy.

In Houston, John is a top man in the 285-man Vinson & Elkins law firm, one of the largest in the country, which occupies six floors in a downtown area building. But Picosa is where his heart is. He likes nothing better than to slip into khakis or jeans, boots and a big hat, saddle up, and spend happy hours helping with the cattle branding and doing honest-to-goodness ranch work.

He has made most of his fortune practicing law and from business, and not from oil, as many people wrongly suppose. And now he's doing modestly well at Picosa, after a long struggle to build it up and reclaim it from the endless thicket of brush and scrub.

"I'm not a bad rancher," he says.

He may be prouder of that than anything he's done so far.

He also sings cowboy ballads—but that subject is one we had better not go into here. ★

Ten miles away from the Picosa Ranch is Floresville, John's birthplace, population around 4,000. You walk around the square there and people you meet say: "Howdy"—omitting the "stranger". They want you to feel at home. There's a restaurant on the edge of town, The Cattleman's Restaurant, open 24 hours a day, which is the town clubhouse. Men slump over a cup of coffee there at all hours, Stetsons pushed back on their heads. And a Sheriff who could double for John Wayne sits there with them, .45 on his left hip—no crime waves in Floresville, you can bet. You can walk around the whole town in minutes, but everyone you meet boasts about how great it is to live there. John's son Mark, president over at the bank, says: "Anyone gets in trouble, and every shop on Main Street will close down to go and help. It's a fine place

to raise a family." Opposite the old courthouse is the tiny Connally For President headquarters. You wouldn't say it's really needed. The whole town is proud of John, and if it comes to that, he's got 4,000-plus votes. ★

John and Nellie Connally have a keen interest in the history of their history-making state of Texas. This marker chronicles the 250-year-old Mission De Las Cabras ("Mission of the Goats"). Below, a peanut and grain warehouse near the Picosa Ranch. Peanuts are big in Wilson County. Bottom photo shows the main drag in Floresville, where they roll up the sidewalks at about 9 p.m. The only action is at "Big Dan's" poolroom and beer emporium, where the tables are jumping to Latin disco records played at deafening decibels. John Connally knows the town well. There are still oldsters around who call him "Johnnie" from the old days and descendants of the Canary Islanders that the Spaniards brought over in 1717 as indentured servants to help tame the land, nod and wave at the man whose line reaches back to Ireland.

Big John is a good man with horses. He is particularly proud of the Galiceno breed his good friend Sid Richardson encouraged him to breed from the stock brought to Yucatan from the Galicia country of Spain by Cortes and the other Spanish conquistadores. Another source of Picosa income is from Coastal Bermuda grass sprigs, which changed things a mighty lot around Picosa. Today the ranch looks as though it's covered in Astroturf. It was not always thus. "Shortly after we started putting the ranch together," Connally tells us, "we were looking for something to stop the erosion. Most of the land in this area is so sandy that its only cover is scrub mesquite and cottonwood, sprouting out of badly eroding red soil. Our land was subject to blowing and bad erosion. Some tracts were blown so badly all you could see was the top of a five-wire fence. So I went in with the Bermuda grass and root planted it myself to about 24 inches deep. It was the first serious plowing that I know about in South Texas. Now we've cleared about 2,500 acres of family land and put it into Coastal Bermuda. From that beginning we developed a business of growing and digging sprigs, and as a consequence there are now millions of acres in South Texas planted with the stuff."★

Standing on its own 3,500 acres atop a hill, the ranch house at Picosa is no log cabin. It is a rambling mansion with a family room 40 feet long and 18 feet high, a fireplace a bear could hibernate in comfortably, an impressive stairway with antique and brass railings, a splendid library filled with handsome volumes and sundry titles, four bedrooms and a high-ceilinged dining room with a 14-foot ebony table and 12 hand-carved chairs. The Connallys like to tell how they bought 90 percent of their furniture at auction, most of it antiques, in Nellie's phrase, of "mixed French Provincial, English and good old American" vintage. The walls are crowded with paintings of Western landscapes, John's favorites.

Nellie mentions with pride the eleven 8-foot doors they have installed around the house, which they purchased in London. "The doors had 40 to 50 coats of varnish on them. We returned them to their natural wood—most of them cypress with oak inserts, but one actually of teakwood."

There's no bell or knocker on the big door at Picosa. If you come as a friend, you just pound on the door with your knuckles—and suddenly there is Nellie opening it, with a smile of welcome as big as all Texas. ★

John's pride and joy at Picosa are his 1,500 Santa Gertrudis. Their massive forms dot the fields of his ranch like great primeval mammals, but they answer every demand of the modern beef market. The Santa Gertrudis is a relatively new strain. Over at the enormous King Ranch in Texas, a spread of a million acres with a cattle population of some 100,000, they were experimenting to improve the steaks yielded by the Texas longhorns. They tried importing Shorthorns and Herefords, but these strains couldn't stand up to Texas weather. The cattle stood around panting in the shade when they should have been grazing. There was the Brahman breed—indifferent to heat and tough fodder and able to sweat like a horse, exuding a substance which acts as an insect repellant—but the Brahman, for some reason, just wouldn't crossbreed with the Shorthorn. Then along came "Monkey," calf of an accidental mating between a carefully nurtured Brahman bull and a plain little old Shorthorn milk cow. The romance had stupendous results. "Monkey" got his monicker because of his playfulness, but when he took to the serious business of growing, he reached a weight of 1,000 pounds in but 12 months. Furthermore, when he was put in with a herd of first-rate Brahman-Shorthorn cows, he produced more than 150 sons, all superior beef animals with the genetic ability to transmit their succulence and hardihood to their offspring. The cherry-red "Monkey" was the sire of a magnificent new breed of cattle, to be called the Santa Gertrudis, after the part of the King Ranch which bore this name from the original Spanish land grant. Today the breed thrives in all of our cattle-raising states and in Australia, South Africa and South America. One stupendous specimen raised by John Connally brought $35,000 at auction. And nature's abundance increases at John's Picosa Ranch every year. ★

John, in the nature of things, can only be a part-time rancher and farmer. But you can tell where his heart is simply by watching him at Picosa. Once upon a time he worked on the family farm, a touch up the road. Now that he's got his own place, it brings out the boy in him again when he's out where his love of the land makes him feel part of it. His feet are on his own soil, and all's right with the world. At left, he surveys his acres with that "look of eagles" so characteristic of him, and which has made many an erring subordinate quail in his boots. His sister, Carmen, says: "John has a deep love for the land. He also has a deep respect for people who work with their hands or who work the land."

Watching him hunker down in his own furrows recalls the words John once spoke to a *Time* magazine reporter while he was being interviewed for a cover story in '64: "One of the things that's meant the most to me is breaking the land with a turning plow. Believe it or not that's a fine sensation. You get under a layer of turf with a plow and it's got sort of a crackle as it breaks loose. I used to take off my shoes because the soil behind the plow just felt good to walk in. It had a good feel, good smell. It had a sort of life to it." ★

The Picosa is run on a full-time basis by a son-in-law, Robert C. Ammann III, who married the former Sharon Connally. Robert is on the near side in the photo (right) with Mark Connally, who lives in Floreville and is president of the First National City Bank of Floresville, in the middle. Like his father, Mark is never happier than when he can get out in those open fields. Below, they are joined by John Connally III, seen at the extreme right of the photograph, who seems to have something to say about the way the others are handling a piece of farm machinery. ★

The men take on the task of unloading feed for the expectant cattle snorting in the background. Big John does his share with a will, getting in licks of physical work which keep him in condition, but which actually are mighty natural to him. At the ranch, the whole family pitches in with the chores, and it isn't unusual for Nellie to whip up a lunch of hamburgers and refried beans. John fancies himself something of an outdoor cook, and cronies who have been out hunting with him—he's known as a pretty good shot with either a scattergun or a rifle—say he's a slick hand with a frying pan. He protects the hunter's role: "There are more mourning doves in Texas today than there were in the days of the Indians."

He likes to fish and enjoys hooking everything upward from pan fish in fresh water to giant sea fighters off the Gulf Coast. "Texas has 4,500 square miles of inland water, it may surprise you to know—more than any other state except Alaska." An ardent conservationist with an overall perspective on wildlife preservation and control, Connally has praised the reestablishment of antelope in Texas as well as the sucessful efforts of landowners to import exotic game such as the axis deer, the mouflon sheep, the black buck antelope and aoudad sheep transplanted from Africa. ★

Commenting on her son's insatiable love of the land, John's mother Lela tells one on the Governor they are still laughing about down in Austin. "John likes to put on old clothes and boots and get around the ranch whenever he can," she says. "One day, I remember, I found him up in one of those big oaks with a pruning saw in his hand. He hadn't been out of the Dallas hospital very long and his arm was still sore." So she ordered the hard-nosed then-Governor of Texas out of the tree. He meekly climbed down.

John shows a lot of interest in driving his tractor, but he remembers the old days, too. "My parents had no electricity until 1940, and I plowed behind mules in Wilson County. When you're from humble surroundings, I think you do your best to become more productive. I'm prepared to plow with mules again if I have to." ★

John has a natural way with kids. Here, he takes quite seriously the observation being made by his granddaughter, Tracy Ammann. Judging by the set of his face, he has some doubts about agreeing with her, however. Below, sampling an apple at a picnic, the look of eagles has flown, and the sour set of his face suggests he is ruminating over the frequent confrontation between farmers and fruit worms. ★

John tests the heft of one of his prize Santa Gertrudis and gives the beast a speculative look. This is a young 'un and nothing like the breed can produce in full-grown specimens, as you can see on the opposite page. The Santa Gertrudis has a marvelous color—the heritage of the cherry-red "Monkey"—which can vary from a deep, almost blood-like color to a lighter tone. As a rule they move with slow dignity, but when one gets his dander up, he can roll like a runaway express train. ★

Two moods of John. Left, thoughtful, contemplating whether the pot has the right proportion of ingredients. (Connally's temper, when he unleashes it, is famous for its fury. The staff at the Governor's mansion is still talking about the day John discovered that they had been putting an unknown brand of coffee in a jar labeled with his favorite kind. His scathing comments nearly took the scalps off of those present and allegedly set the pot boiling without turning on the heat.) Below, a king in all his glory, one of the Connally Santa Gertrudis bulls virtually blocks out his proud owners with his sovereign bulk. Even in their evening clothes, which is the way you dress in Texas to go to a topnotch cattle auction, the Connally clan (note John beaming over the massive rump) had to take a back seat on this occasion, and gladly, too—this beast brought a price of $35,000. ★

Once again, the Connallys stand back (left) as Mark makes a point to his father about an aspect of the cattle pens and their brooding inmates. A good animal can top 2,600 pounds on the hoof, and the one in the foreground may well be close to that. Below, Connally, the amateur veterinarian, takes a close look at one of his ranch horses. While a youth, John rode a horse five miles to school and back every day. He's a good horseman, even by Texas standards. ★

John Connally spends many of his quiet hours meditating (left) on the problems currently infesting our country's economy and devising strategy for strengthening our declining image in the world community.

In his less quiet hours he may be found (below) joining the happy festivities of his vivacious grandchildren. Here, the littlest "angel" holds the floor—and her proud grandpa's eye. ★

John III, John and Mark Connally talk things over in front of a curious bunch of Santa Gertrudis, who may be wondering why the three don't stand up like most humans do. Even on the ranch, father John is very much the take-charge type of guy. John III says: "Dad makes most of the ranch decisions. He's still the patriarch of the family, and there has always been lots of communication between us. We've always been a very close family—closer than most." ★

John Connally's view: "I don't have a single minded approach to life, and so I've done well at a number of things. I think, for example, I'm a pretty good rancher. Not mediocre, and I could be great at it if I had worked at it all the time." Success runs in the Connally family. Below, a proud John stands beside son Mark in front of the Floresville Bank where the younger Connally serves as president. ★

Nellie

The girl that John married after he met her at college, then Idanell Brill, is today a radiant, attractive woman—an eye-catcher wherever she goes.

I spent some time with her the day after last Thanksgiving at their favorite Texas retreat, the Picosa Ranch, which, strangely enough, for all its lordly 6,000 acreage, splendid furnishings and herds of great animals, is still what the Texans call a "spread"—meaning it's a place where a man feels at home because it is *his* home.

Nellie is, well . . . just Nellie. She could well be John Connally's greatest asset. The coed who was as cute as a bug in a rug in 1935 and won all those "sweetheart" elections is still very much in evidence in her good figure, curly hair, natural grooming and vibrant good health. With it all she is serene and composed, a person at peace with herself and the world.

Just outside of the ranch front door is a stone sculpture Nellie created by grouping some natural rock into a creative and pleasant shape. It's *good*—not just because it's hers, but because it tells something about her taste, her feeling for nature, for strength, for unity of form. The interior of the ranch is the same: good taste, comfortable good taste.

Connally once admitted: "I have an insatiable curiosity about everything. I try to learn something about everything I do." And in this Nellie is just like him. "We are both interested in art," says John, "paintings, sculpture, books, in

the outdoors and wildlife. We love to travel—to see not only the scenery but also the people—and there's a lot in this world to see."

Especially at her ranch, Nellie radiates her happiness. "We had 15 at the table," she said that day after Thanksgiving, "two in high chairs." She meant: "How many and how *good!*" She loves to be among her family, and never more than when she—a fabulous cook—is whipping up some special new recipe for them in the kitchen.

In this world of givers and takers, as you leave Nellie, you shake your head a bit at how wonderful it was to be with her, how quick she is to respond, how simple and direct her speech is. That is because Nellie is a "life giver" and always has been, to judge by the way Texans —and these days hordes of others—idolize her.

She might well treasure something her son Mark said to me about her. After commenting on how his father and mother had never let politics interfere with their duties as parents in caring for their children (when the couple left Washington in 1962 for Connally to run for Governor in Texas, Nellie extracted a promise from him that they would not go back to D.C. until their children had all finished high school), Mark paused a moment—he was sitting at his desk in the bank in Floresville—and summed it all up, quickly:

"My mother is a great lady."

I agree. ★

John Connally has learned to separate his private life from his political ambitions—a real achievement for any public figure. John gives Nellie credit for this: "She was always more interested in protecting our privacy than she has been in favor of my aspiring to political office or political fame."

Nellie has done more than that.

Looking back on that terrible day in Dallas when he was caught in the cross fire of the assassin who killed President Kennedy, John Connally—the man who can say "I have memories shared by no other man"—recalls:

"Nellie saved me, I know that. The bullet split my lung, but Nellie pulled my head into her lap and, when she did it, closed the opening in my chest. I was bleeding profusely and was actually dying." Then Nellie brought her body around so as to cover her husband's body with her own and catch in his stead any more bullets intended for him. John's words before he lapsed into unconsciousness were: "Somebody take care of Nellie."

And now today, by the grace of God, someone is. His first name is John. ★

Any caption writer looking at this absolutely enchanting photograph of Nellie and John Connally should simply shut down his typewriter and go away whistling "Love's Old, Sweet Song." But fortunately, both of them have said words that fit the music perfectly. Says John: "Nellie has influenced my life more than anybody. We've been married more than 39 years and it has been as nearly a perfect marriage as I can imagine. We've had fewer unpleasant moments than almost anybody in the world." Says Nellie as she snuggles up to her husband, driving a carryall down the ranch roads she has painstakingly lined with Pyracantha: "I can't remember when I didn't know John Connally." ★

72

Nellie and John like nothing better than a family reunion, and what a family it is! These pictures show the joy of their get-togethers and how they treasure each other's company. The cluster below is centered by a giant statue honoring the humble peanut, the agricultural staple of Wilson County, which stands proud and solid on the lawn of the county courthouse in Floresville.★

She said to me in touching seriousness: "John and I have examined all the candidates for the Presidency with great care. Believe me, if we could find one who had the experience and the capabilities which make him a better man than John, we would turn all our energies and efforts to helping elect him. But there are important things at stake here. John's concern is not for the office alone—he cares about the world all of us are going to turn over to generations to come. We both know he is the man to do it. And don't forget, he has never lost in running for an office he wanted. It could happen some day, of course, but not because he ran with the tide. Win or lose, he says what he stands firm for, and then lets the votes fall where they may." ★

Nellie and John like to do things together, whether it is heading up an inaugural ball at the Governor's mansion in Austin or just enjoying the flowers dancing under the oaks. Nellie laughs in glee at the memory of a feminist reporter who once asked her if she regretted not having any career of her own. "My career is being a wife and mother, and it's one I wouldn't change for anything. It's a man's world, and you need a niche or a spot of your own. My finest joy is in my family and my children. I married a very public man. He won't ever retire. Politics is part of him. He has great concern for his country, his state and his grandchildren."

She pauses, and Nellie is not above winking at you when she wants to. "We discuss things freely, and I give advice whether I'm asked for it or not. The world may not be aware of it, but I have a mind of my own." ★

Nellie is always there to come forth with a crumpet or wipe away a tear to keep the world of her grandchildren in bright array. But in one sense, the children around her are all children everywhere. The Connallys' first son, John, and his wife named their little daughter Nell, much to the delight of her grandmother. ★

Campaign

John believes in politics. He enjoys politics. He thinks that every man, woman and child should participate in public affairs of the community, the state and the nation. He says simply:

"I think it's not only a privilege, it's a firm obligation and a firm duty. I don't think there is a higher obligation or a higher duty—except your reverence to the Almighty God."

Would you take a man who said that and make him stand at factory gates and shake the hand of everyone who comes out when the whistle blows? Profess undying admiration for hordes of women in hair curlers whom he will never see again? Kiss babies and kids, no matter how flubbered and flabbered they might be, as if they were heaven's own cherubs? Walk into supermarkets and interrupt people in their shopping with impromptu speeches on the Middle East, energy and the cost of lamb chops? Would you make "pressing the flesh" one of the higher callings?

No, you wouldn't—but you do. His reward for political principles (and he must have them to willingly undergo the tortures of the national cult exercise we indulge in every four years called the campaign trail) is an ordeal in travel, speechmaking, merciless publicity and an occasional merciless hostility, laced with rubber-chicken dinners at a thousand dollars and intermittent dosages of shashlik, bagels, corned beef and cabbage, hominy grits, maple syrup, venison steak, pork, spaghetti, and every other conceivable kind of food in order to demonstrate ethnic impartiality to everyone and everything except his own gastric juices.

John Connally, who knows full well his intensity, good looks and brain power have an electric effect on most people, is stressing leadership. "We haven't leadership today; I wish we did." The well-known fact that he switched parties he apparently uses as a possible advantage. "Some Republicans are elated that I am in the party, and others view me as a newcomer....I know that the most militant Democrats resent the fact that I switched parties and view me with disdain, if not hate. But the average Democrat is a vote-switcher himself."

Connally feels that he uniquely fits the mold of the candidate people endorse when they say: "I vote for the individual, not the party."

John is quite an individual, that's for sure. And on that, he is staking his political fate in 1980. ★

And the people—what of the people?

John comes across to them as someone who speaks his mind, and no foolin'.

And he reaches them.

A prominent Texan once said this about him: "His traits of personality go beyond the term *charisma* in my view. He's a much more complex individual that comes through just in that sort of a term. I think his depth and his accomplishments and his stature go far beyond the theory of charisma. He certainly has that. He is a most dynamic and attractive individual to both sexes. . . . To men he treats himself in such a light that it is very easy to follow him because he is so articulate, so dynamic and generally so correct in his judgment. As far as women are concerned, his looks, his stature, his physical bearing, his warmth . . . all come through to the opposite sex. They have naturally the same admiration for his character that men have.

"John Connally is a leader—a strong, articulate, charismatic leader. He is able to sway to his way of thinking most people, even though they may have been originally opposed to his ideas . . . what he truly is, is a man of the nation and of the world." ★

80

In the Watergate era this man, "Jake" Jacobsen, was in deep trouble in Texas. He was accused and was later convicted of misappropriating $825,000. Plea-bargaining for a light sentence, he accused Connally of accepting a $10,000 bribe . Connally had been Nixon's Secretary of Treasury, so he was fair game for the Watergate special prosecutor. A Washington, D.C., jury said Connally was innocent of all charges. Today no credible shred of evidence can be found of this $10,000 "bribe." It is now known that the campaign funds of a host of other politicians *had* accepted "milk money." Connally at the time was not running for office. He was a millionaire many times over. The charge that he would accept a $10,000 pittance from a man as shady as Jacobsen is ludicrous. Jacobsen, as promised, was lightly sentenced to but seven years probation. He might have gone to prison for 40 years. ★

People like the way John comes right to the point: "I was over in Europe recently and folks there were taking pity on me because of the country I came from. I don't like to be pitied. I want a country that's on top again." He anticipates the questions that are going to be asked about his switching parties, and he takes the bull by the horns and lets them know about it in his talk before they even ask: "It's immaterial which party I'm in because I never play my cards for personal advancement politically. I have responded solely to my own philosophy in my career. The point was, and is, that the Democrats and their leadership are on a program of more spending, deficit spending and more government control. Bureaucracy is wrong and I wouldn't want to be President and have to advocate any program like that. That is why I quit the Democrats.... Every day that passes convinces me more that I was right and that I made the right decision. I think the Democratic party has veered to a path that is absolutely and completely wrong and detrimental to the best interests of the country. Jimmy Carter got where he is by promising many things to many people—more government planning, more government control, more government intervention—and I just don't believe in it. There is no way I could have been the nominee of the Democratic party." John comes out swinging, too, on the subject of the "milk fund scandal," where he was accused of accepting a $10,000 persuader to use his influence in Washington to keep the price of milk up. He says it was pinned on him by a man who testified against him only to avoid prosecution for embezzlement. "He never gave me a dime. I never took a dime for anything in my life and I'd *never* do it. They haven't printed enough money to buy me.... I stood trial in Washington, D.C., in a political environment where 83 percent of the people voted for George McGovern in 1972, where the jury was composed primarily of women, 10 out of 12 were black, and they said: *'Not guilty! Not guilty!'* Now, what more do you want?"... "I think everyone now agrees I got a bum rap. I was framed. Sure I'll talk about the trial. The jury said I was innocent." ★

John and Nellie swing along in a parade, and although they are the only ones on foot, a jaunty wave of the hand and a big smile get the idea over that they are a couple of good skates, too.

But these campaign days, it isn't all smiles and waves. John gets back to the message of opportunity he has: "Nothing is more critical than the restoration of confidence of the people in our form of government. I know of nothing that would be more conducive to that restoration than the knowledge that an American President has, from the day of his assumption of office, fulfilled his political role and has no future except as historians view him as a statesman. I believe there still is a greater destiny ahead for our nation. I believe we can have renewed hope for a greater future for our people." ★

John calls a spade a spade: "My natural inclination is to support the President, whoever he is. I believe that President Carter is a sincere, patriotic, hard-working man who wants very much to have a successful administration. But these qualities are insufficient to provide effective leadership when an administration lacks the national and international perspective to cope with the multitude of problems that confront the United States and the world. The Carter Administration is wrong for the times in which we live. It has little sense of strategy and little sense of the use of power on a global scale. Abroad and at home, the nation simply cannot afford four more years of this administration." ★

John, appearing everywhere he can for national publicity, addresses Tom Brokaw on the "Today Show." Regardless of their conversation he never minds getting down to specifics, as he has said so often: "More leadership should be shown in the development of energy policies. We cannot indefinitely continue a 50 percent dependence on foreign oil. Our national security is at stake. Our balance of trade is in a deepening deficit. The greatest and most advanced nation on earth is a debtor to the OPEC cartel—and too little is being done about it. And we have been twice warned—in 1973 and again with the Iranian crisis. We have to produce more coal and use more coal. We have to provide incentive for the greater exploration and the development of oil and gas. And we have to build more nuclear power plants. We may have to revise the mining laws.

"We may have to revise the environmental restraints. We have to provide the balance that permits the nation to survive economically while we make progress environmentally. But, today, there is no national energy policy except in name. We know it—and the world knows it. This is but one example of government mistrust of free enterprise." ★

$\mathbf{J}$ohn, shown here with Nellie and his brother Merrill, simply exudes confidence wherever he goes. He is what some people call a "life-giver"—after contact with him you go away feeling recharged by his contagious energy and self-assurance.

"It is time to signal the world that the United States is strong and resourceful, resolving its own problems and meeting its responsibility for peace and freedom. Indeed, our nation is basically strong. But it has a developing image of weakness. It is time to portray the true image of America to the rest of the world—and, just as important, to our own citizens who have lost so much confidence in their government." ★

The "press" is predominately liberal. Frequently it has been outright hostile to John Connally. Political writers misinterpret John's nononsense approach that "if we want more we must produce more" as being against the poor. They fail to note that John Connally once was poor and knows how the poor want to be treated. For decades, past Presidents have noted Connally's Presidential qualities. The press has been slower but it's coming around. *The Saturday Evening Post* featured John on the cover in November 1978 and bravely predicted, "There's a tide running . . . which could carry him as far as the White House in 1980."

Also in the fall of 1978, the bucolic *Country Gentleman* had a Connally cover story. It pointed out the key to Connally's character was his love of the soil and his abiding faith in the land.

Time magazine ran a Connally cover story in the September 10, 1979, issue. One decided plus in the article: It crisply laid the so-called "milk fund scandal" to rest.

Last November the prestigious *New York Times* put Connally on the cover of its weekly magazine and carried a detailed analysis inside written by Steven Brill. The article is critical (it stresses Connally's connections with business) but fair. Obviously the *Times* believes Connally is a contender who may well last the course. The press has come to believe in the Connally magic. ★

THE SATURDAY EVENING POST

14250

Nov. '78 $1.25

Nancy
Lopez
Smiles

"Baby
Transplants"
from
Fertile
Eggs

John B.
Connally:
Strong
for 1980

NEW

BY

SEPTEMBER 10, 1979 $1.25

TIME

Hot
on the
Trail

G.O.P. Candidate
John Connally

untry Gentleman

Fall, 1978   The Magazine of Country Living $1.25

COMING
ON TOUGH
Presidential
Candidate
John Connally

89

The press has tried to dub John Connally a "Wheeler Dealer." His reply to that accusation leveled at him on the CBS Evening News was "If it means somebody that knows how to sit across the negotiating table from Leonid Brezhnev or a Helmut Schmidt or a Prime Minister Ohira, I sure can do that and not come out second best in the trade, in my judgment. Now, if that is what they mean, I'll plead guilty to all that."

He says, "If it means I could go into the Senate and get some legislation enacted, I'm guilty.

"If it means I could enter a horse trade and come out without losing, I guess I'm guilty." ★

Last October 12, long before the Soviet invasion of Afghanistan, John Connally called for a strong military presence in the Middle East. This major address has been lauded by responsible Middle East authorities everywhere. However, the press missed his major points and aroused criticism by taking one small part out of context. Anticipating this, the Connally for President Committee placed an advertisement of the entire address in the *Washington Post*. Connally feels that unless the United States maintains military strength sufficient to keep the peace, there is no hope for Israel anyway. They have to look to us for protection. Says Connally, "You cannot purge fear and suspicion from the minds of people on both sides. And you cannot eliminate the ever-present danger. Therefore a strong military presence is essential."★

THE WASHINGTON POST

Friday, October 12, 1979

Paid Political Advertisement

JOHN CONNALLY PROPOSES A NEW APPROACH TO BUILD STABILITY AND LASTING PEACE IN THE MIDDLE EAST.

Complete text of an address by Republican Presidential Candidate John B. Connally to the Washington Press Club on October 11, 1979.

Connally for President Committee
3110 Columbia Pike, Arlington, Virginia 22204 • (703) 892-3500

Left, while a Connally supporter smilingly observes the effect on his pretty young daughter, John doesn't even have to work at charming this young lady. Obviously, she agrees that he looks just like the President she's always had in mind for her country.★

91

John stands out in a crowd, any crowd. These days sometimes it may seem that he is telling them what they want to hear, but the truth of the matter is that he is speaking for himself and letting the cards fall where they may. It could just be, however, that the two are one and the same—if this is a man whose thoughts and attitudes are in the right place at the right time. "After 60 years of power, the communist system in Russia has been tried and found wanting. Our own system, whatever its faults, provides a better life, both materially and spiritually. We are economically stronger than the Soviet Union. Militarily we can be as strong as we need to be as long as we need to be. The only missing ingredient is leadership—mobilizing our resources, building the free economic system with its tradition of individual freedom, maintaining a strong defense and working with our allies for the preservation of peace. In recent years the Soviet Union has embarked upon an intensified policy of expansion which threatens that peace. Today it is concentrating on Africa, the Persian Gulf area and Southeast Asia. I believe it is time for a strong President to make it clear that this policy is not acceptable." ★

John knows how to put it to them. Some of his opponents read careful statements prepared by others for them. Others try to speak extemporaneously and get lost in a jungle of words; not he. He looks up, catches their attention with those blue eyes and talks straight from the shoulder: "I am an optimist. I believe in this country. I believe in the basic good sense of the American people, people who are tired of being treated like children who don't know what's best for them—treated like children by politicians and bureaucrats who may be sincere in their desire to run our lives but who have lost their understanding of what makes America great. I am optimistic enough to believe that type of leadership in America is passé and outmoded—a useless relic of bygone days. It is out of date—irrelevant to the future of America—and the sooner it disappears the sooner the American people will begin working in concert again for the health and security of our country. We are told by the President that there is a crisis of confidence in America. I agree. There can be little doubt that the people have lost a great deal of confidence in our political leadership. But I believe it can be easily regained at such time as our leadership has earned it."★

John Connally pledged early in his campaign to actively pursue the Presidential nomination in all 50 states. At right, he swaps views with avid supporters in Iowa. Below, he dons black tie and tux to accept the honor of being named "Man of the Year" by the Chicago Boys Club. After his prepared remarks, John took time to say a special "thank you" to a proud member of the youth organization. ★

F loresville, Texas, may be fertile ground for peanuts but it definitely isn't Carter country. A supporter in John Connally's home town doesn't pass up the opportunity to capitalize on a ready-made situation. And his message comes through loud and clear. ★

"The time for timid approaches is long past. The fabric of Western security is like an old carpet. It is threadbare in some places, broken in others and stretched everywhere. We must start by casting out the devil of defeatism and recapturing the dynamism that once made this country the world's first superpower." ★

Even in the hubbub and excitement and hoopla of campaigning John never takes his eye off the ball: "We are in a struggle for nothing less than global leadership—not only a struggle for the resources of the world within which all economic progress is rooted, but also a struggle for the minds of men in which the tree of freedom is rooted. We are in an economic war. We are in a political war. We are in a propaganda war. We are in a psychological war. None of these conflicts is especially pleasant to contemplate. . . ." ★

Above, John Connally talks with farmers at a Farm Bureau meeting in Des Moines, Iowa. Connally has outlined his agricultural program assuring farmers he would revise the Commodity Corporation Credit structure to encourage foreign nations to buy more grain, red meat and poultry. He would also revise Title I of Public Law 480, agriculture aid to underdeveloped nations, to expand demand for U.S. grain in the Third World. He would allow the American farmer to store more of his own grain by revising provisions of the loan program. And lastly, use the public sector and the private sector to find new markets for American agricultural goods. ★

The electorate is made up of individuals, and no one knows this better than the candidate with the perfect record of victory. Left, he shakes hands and engages in a little low-key campaigning with diehard supporters and on-the-fence observers. Dispelling misconceptions about their candidate is a never-ending task for Connally workers. "I wouldn't vote for him because he's just another Lyndon Johnson," complains a detractor. Connally enthusiasts are quick to point out that their man left Johnson's camp because he couldn't convince Lyndon that the Great Society give-away programs would never work while we were expecting our young men to sacrifice their lives in the Viet Nam war. He disagreed with many of the liberal Johnson programs. ★

"The American people traditionally have preferred to live and let live, enjoying the fruits of our hard-won freedoms and trusting the example we set will enable those freedoms to bloom and blossom in the far reaches of the world. So we are ill-equipped to engage in these conflicts. We are being forced to rethink our strategy.

At home and abroad, America has been mortgaging its future rather than investing in it. We have been living off past technological excellence and myths of unsurpassable military superiority on the one hand, and off a dwindling margin of renewable and unrenewable resources on the other." ★

"At home we have failed to stem inflation and failed to cope successfully with the energy problem. Abroad we have drawn down on our hard-earned capital of respect and prestige and are now being challenged both economically and politically by friend and foe alike. It would help, of course, if we would stop fumbling our opportunities and seize some advantages when they are ripe for the taking...." ★

Though his financial support is coming from business, and not all of it *big*, Connally is a grass-roots candidate. The young, the old, the successful and the aspiring flock to John for leadership. As one voice they cheer his dedication, laud his accomplishments and emulate his optimism. It comforts them to hear a politician think as they think. "It is the *middle-class* that is forgotten. They're the ones taking it in the neck. And I *am* going to speak for them." As Texas' Governor, Connally stressed helping people help themselves by providing jobs for all and vocational training for those not in the labor force. ★

Leadership, confidence, restoration. John invites the voters to join him: "The American people have never been a nation of quitters or hand-wringers. Once we clearly see the nature of a crisis we have always risen to the challenge. Today we must say to the world: We are ready to regain control over our own destiny; we are ready to face reality; we are ready to act with courage when the occasion demands. Five years from now I hope to come back here, meet with you again and be able to say that I have been able to lead America back to the road of international recovery. With your help, and the support of your neighbors and millions of Americans, there is no reason why we cannot keep our appointment." ★

Where will it all end? The art of pressing the flesh is still the politician's best weapon, other than his words, to get the message of his human spirit across to the millions of voters out there. John Connally is indefatigable, hopeful and confident not only in pressing the flesh but in pressing his message to all people. He sums it all in one word—LEADERSHIP.

He's got it, he says, exuberantly.

And, in the Presidential sense, only time will tell. ★

Issues

The well-tested conventional wisdom about how to run for President is to patch together, and use over and over, one general all-purpose political speech that has plenty of shining phrases but is essentially so shallow that it tells the voters virtually nothing about what you would do if elected. It is a technique which sometimes seems to work. The pollsters can commune with their computers for a few minutes and show you exactly what sentiments, fears, hopes and irritations can just now be most advantageously stirred by campaign oratory—and what key phrases to use. The trick is to project a favorable image that seems to reflect the feelings of most voters and wins their support, but doesn't commit you to anything except peace, prosperity and the family farm.

This pretested packaging of candidates by the new breed of campaign managers is by now well understood. It is widely used by both Democrats and Republicans, by both liberals and conservatives, by such seemingly opposite types as Ronald Reagan and Teddy Kennedy.

But not by John Connally.

Governor Connally has taken the daring view that the voters want to be talked to about the real issues—and talked to straight. He has had the courage to say what he thinks and what he would do about some of the toughest issues this country faces. In a series of bold, candid statements, early in his campaign, he took up directly and decisively some of the hard problems other candidates in both parties had been dodging or double-talking their way around. To him a most fundamental requirement of personal integrity is

to let people know who you are and where you stand. People know where John Connally stands on the major issues. He planned that they should. Here are some of those issues and a summary of what Connally has had to say about them:

The Middle East

Of all the hard and controversial issues an American President or Presidential candidate has had to face during the past 30 years, nothing has been more difficult, more complicated, more laden with deep emotional overtones, more wired with political booby traps than the issue of the Middle East. America's special ties with Israel since the day it was recognized as a state in May 1948, the passionate commitment of American Jews to the welfare of Israel, the links of Israeli intelligence with U.S. military intelligence, America's dependence on Arab-controlled Middle East oil, and the rivalry of the U.S. and the U.S.S.R. for predominant influence in that vital area—all these factors have made the defining and executing of a fair, coherent and consistent American policy in the Middle East almost impossible.

The cynical judgment of many observers of the international scene, in Washington and abroad, has been for years that an American President can deal objectively with the gut issues of the Arab-Israeli conflict only during about the first 18 months of his administration, and that no candidate dare talk about the issues in other than bland and simplistic terms. American candidates for office have become extraordinarily skillful in giving convoluted speeches designed to reassure the Israelis, to keep the Arabs quiet (and willing to go on shipping us oil), and to warn the Russians to stand back. It is a very tricky performance to bring off. In the last few years there have been growing ominous signs that this game cannot be played successfully any longer.

The war of October 1973, in which the Egyptians drove the Israelis back from the Suez Canal and the Syrians regained a sizeable chunk of their land on the northern front—even though the Israelis later "won" the war—shocked Israel and her supporters profoundly. The Arabs proved that they could and would fight effectively, and for the first time the Arabs used their "oil weapon" by curtailing sales to the United States and other industrialized nations. From that time on the Middle East could never be the same again. The no peace/no war stalemate, with Israel holding the upper hand, could not be indefinitely prolonged. That was becoming clear even before President Anwar el Sadat made his historic trip to Jerusalem in November 1977, before the Camp David accords and the subsequent Egyptian-Israeli peace treaty was signed, and before the P.L.O. and the Palestinian homeland issue had attracted such broad international attention.

Still, all sensible, cautious, traditional American candidates could be expected to duck and dodge and weave whenever key Middle East issues were thrown at them.

But not John Connally.

On October 11, 1979, at the National Press Club in Washington, he stood up before one of the most critical, politically sophisticated audiences in America and laid out a daring, detailed plan for a comprehensive Middle East peace. He did that despite the fact that he had every reason to expect that his words would be distorted, that other candidates would try to twist his forthright words so as to damage him with Jewish voters, and that, at the very least, he would be accused of "recklessness." What did he say?

He said that the United States must give continued "support for Israel's security—which is a moral imperative" and must induce the Arabs to "finally accept Israel's sovereignty and territorial integrity." But he also said that Israel would have

to withdraw from the Palestinian Arab territories in the West Bank, Gaza and the Golan Heights that they seized in June 1967 and have held under military occupation ever since. At the same time, he insisted, these territories would have to be demilitarized after they are returned to the Palestinians, except for military strong points Israel should be able to "lease" for an agreed-upon period of time.

Connally also said that Israel would have to withdraw the controversial Israeli civilian settlements that had been planted in various parts of the occupied Palestinian districts and which, up to now, all U.S. administrations have regarded as "illegal" and as an "obstacle to peace." Even so, he qualified this recommendation with the proposal that such evacuation should be on a "phased basis" after evidence of "good faith is established," and that Israel should receive financial assistance for this resettlement.

He advocated that the Palestinians should be allowed to exercise their right of self-determination and self-government, but indicated his preference that these rights should be realized in some close relationship with Jordan, an idea previously expressed by many Israelis. On the exceedingly thorny question of the future of Jerusalem, he proposed that Jerusalem should remain united, with "free circulation" throughout, with "unimpeded access" for each religious community to all its holy places and with "substantial political autonomy" for each of the national (Jewish and Palestinian Arab) groups in the city.

He also came out for a custom union between Israel and any future Palestinian homeland, plus a joint Israeli-Palestinian "development bank" to assist both peoples.

Going beyond the question of Israeli-Palestinian relations, Governor Connally proposed that simultaneous with the conclusion of a comprehensive peace settlement, Saudi Arabia and other oil-producing Arab states should be induced to make commitments concerning "stable oil supplies" and the renunciation of the "oil weapon."

To guarantee the carrying out of a comprehensive peace agreement and to prevent Soviet adventurism, he called for major, prompt and decisive actions by the United States to create "a strong military presence" in the area to "provide a military shield for our Middle East interests."

Practically everything Connally said in that speech had been advocated at one time or another by previous Presidents and Secretaries of State and by concerned diplomats and Middle East specialists from various Free World countries. Moreover, what he proposed was entirely in accord with the letter and spirit of United Nations Resolution 242, adopted unanimously by the Security Council in November 1967 and repeatedly referred to by all states that are parties to the dispute as the agreed-upon basis for a Middle East peace.

What Governor Connally did, however, that upset some people was challenge his fellow Americans and the world to move beyond declarations of broad principles and empty promises—and to act. He warned that time is running out in the Middle East, that it is the most volatile area in the world and that the longer real peace is delayed the greater the hazards to the United States, to Israel and the other peoples of the area and to the whole world.

Most of those who criticized Governor Connally for his forthright analysis of the Middle East problem did not so much disagree with the substance of what he said. They quarrelled with his timing, with the comprehensive linking together of various elements in his plan and with his sense of urgency.

Yet despite the attacks made on his Middle East peace plan, the mail responses, according to his aides, were clearly favorable at about a four-to-one ratio. Although a number of Jewish leaders were initially upset, some, after carefully reading the text of his statement, reported that they felt his proposals made sense and would have to be faced up to sooner or later.

On this, as on certain other major issues, John Connally is convinced that the really great problems don't just solve themselves, that delay in dealing with them is no policy, that silence brings no answers and that leadership requires realistic and informed thinking, straight talk and courageous deeds. He believes that the long-festering Middle East conflict can be solved and must be solved. He demands that we get on with it—now.

The Economy

Governor Connally has spoken frequently and incisively about the numerous and many-layered problems of the American economy. He has presented repeatedly a sobering account of the assorted ills to which our economy has fallen prey: runaway inflation, a collapsing dollar, declining productivity, huge foreign trade deficits, perennially unbalanced budgets and loss of faith, at home and abroad, in the capacity of the U.S. government to deal with the nation's economic ills.

Like most candidates, Governor Connally has called for a balanced federal budget. But he has gone on to spell out how the tax code should be changed so that more investment, more jobs, more production, more income can be brought about. Only by greater production, fuller use of our manpower and womanpower, can we hope to curb inflation, eliminate the foreign trade deficit, strengthen the dollar and generate the income from which taxes can be drawn to balance the budget. To move the economy in that direction, he proposes some concrete revisions in the tax laws to provide greater incentives for savings and productive investments. Specifically, he urges that the tax code be amended to allow each taxpayer to create an individual "taxpayer's nest egg" account of, perhaps, up to $10,000 that would be protected from federal taxation as long as it should be invested and regardless of possible shifts from one form of investment to another. Such an arrangement would produce an immediate large-scale increase in the pool of capital for research and new plant development, something American industry desperately needs to hold its own in the markets of the world. (It would also introduce an element of greater fairness into the tax system by giving lower- and middle-income taxpayers some of the tax shelter benefits long enjoyed by the more affluent.)

Governor Connally points out that although political leaders in both parties have often advocated a higher rate of saving by the American people, supportive action has been lacking. The pressure of inflation produces a psychology of spend-now-before-the-prices-go-higher, and the tax laws provide no incentives for saving. The result is that Americans put a smaller percentage of their earnings into savings than almost any other industrialized nation. No wonder we have a "capital formation" problem. Governor Connally believes that that situation can be corrected not by "jaw-boning" the public to buy more government bonds but by giving practical incentives to invest in the improvement of the American productive plant.

The modernization of that plant, he believes, must be given high priority in any plan for the strengthening of the economy. To that end he advocates increased investment incentives for business firms, as well as the untaxed "nest egg" arrangement for individuals.

"We should encourage businesses," he has said, "to build the buildings, purchase the equipment and buy the trucks and cars that generate new jobs." That encouragement promptly and effectively given by allowing a rapid tax write-off of these investments—ten years for new buildings, five years for equipment, three years for automotive vehicles, and one year for plant improvements—could be "dictated by the federal government."

In providing more incentives for everyone to save and invest, Connally has said, "We are offering a stimulus to the economy that leads to greater productivity without the plague of runaway inflation.

"We create vast new capital urgently needed to rebuild and modernize American industry—to make it more competitive in world markets and to thereby create more jobs—and that's the way to create more productivity, the ultimate answer to inflation.

"We cannot spend our way out of our economic problems, but we can certainly save and invest our way out."

The Governor likes to point out that the private sector provides five out of every six jobs held by Americans and, therefore, a healthy, vigorous, expanding private sector is the best guarantee that the needs of the poor, the elderly and the handicapped will be cared for. He rejects the notion that the problems of the underprivileged will be solved just by throwing more government money at them.

He wants to see a cap placed on federal expenditures and is convinced that the mood of the people, increasingly reflected in the Congress, will make it possible for a new President to set and hold to reduced limits on government spending. Our basic trouble for years, he says, is that we have been suffering from "runaway politics." We have proceeded in "undisciplined" fashion, with unrealistic promises of what the government could do for virtually everybody. That era of "economic irresponsibility," he insists, has to end.

John Connally does not promise quick, easy answers to these economic difficulties, however. He predicts that even with sound economic policies restored it will take "at the very minimum, two to four years . . . to bring inflation under reasonable control."

He warns that "the easy times are over. Cheap land, cheap housing, cheap food, cheap transportation, cheap health, cheap education, even cheap leisure are part of the past. A new American politics is required, a politics which is honest with itself and honest with the people in acknowledging that promises and performances can no longer carry a cheap price."

Alongside these austere warnings, Connally sets forth a low-key argument for a substantial tax cut for both individuals and corporations. The reason, he makes clear, is not for short-term political effect, but for the sake of long-term economic stimulation. Here again, he reverts to his favorite theme: that the rate of growth in American manufacturing productivity must be increased. Our rate of growth has been under 3 percent for more than a decade; Japan's has been three times as great, and we have also been outstripped by Germany, France, Canada and even Great Britain.

"This performance by our American economy," says Connally, "is intolerable." He makes it clear that his top priority in dealing with the economy is to promote "healthy, anti-inflationary growth . . . in American industry."

Agriculture

Agriculture is no different from Connally's

other major policy areas. He leaves no question as to where he stands.

Coming from a farm background, and being the owner and operator of 9,000 acres of Texas ranch land, Connally has an acute understanding of the problems that face the American farmer today.

Farmers are small-business men plagued by the economy. Money is tight, and if it is available the cost of farming is prohibitive. As a result, the machinery, tools and seed that the farmer buys to plant and harvest his crops have become ever more difficult to obtain.

Connally tells farmers across the nation that "while Americans are called upon not to borrow money, not to start a small business, not to buy a combine or tractor, the federal government disciplines itself not at all, continuing to print and spend money as if there is no tomorrow."

Energy is a major concern to everyone, but it is especially important to the farmer. Without adequate energy, agriculture will suffer, and the ripple effect on the economy will be enormous. Consider that agriculture trade reaped a $16 billion surplus last year, the largest of any segment of American production.

Threats of inadequate fuel, diesel and gasoline have already caused farmers problems in many parts of the country. Connally's policies would alleviate these problems by "freeing the genius of private enterprise," as in the Midwest's attempt to increase "gasohol" supplies.

Connally also proposes that we share our energy technology and expertise with Mexico and Canada in return for increased fuels from these two countries. (This is a part of Connally's North American Common Market Policy.)

Transportation is another problem facing the American farmer. Connally proposes that a stronger transportation system be developed in the years ahead. One that will "insure all potential goods to arrive at the marketplace intact and on time." It is estimated that in 1979 alone, close to one and a half billion dollars in agricultural income will be lost due to transportation shortages.

Connally says that we have to deal with these problems and do much more.

"We have to see that more foreign markets are opened to American goods and products. The more we export, the more profits we accrue. The more profits rise, the more opportunity beckons, both on and off the farm."

He says we have to "discourage blatant protectionist policies espoused by countries against whom we compete," and at the same time heighten the competitive nature of our products abroad; encourage our rivals to lessen excessive savings rates; take full advantage, as many of our European colleagues have, of those few import relaxations allowed by nations like Japan."

Also, Connally says, we have to encourage companies to reinvest profits in new plants, new equipment and new research and development aided by a "government which seeks to make us more successful in foreign markets and more employable at home."

"Farmers are feeding America and the world, and feeding it well," Connally tells a group of farmers in Minnesota. Consumers in the late '50s paid 24 percent of their disposable income for food. Today they pay only 16 percent. Farmers are also producing close to 65 percent of the edible grain in the world, as compared to 43 percent 20 years ago.

Connally asks the group, "How was all this made possible? Not through government subsidy. Not through endless bounty issued from Washington, D.C. Not through government giving more to people, but through people giving more of themselves." Farmers do this. They represent what is right in America. They produce grain and livestock in more abundance than any nation in the world. Few segments of American industry are as competitive. Connally's answer to keeping it that way is the free enterprise system and hard work.

Finally, Governor Connally feels additional substantive measures must be taken immediately to assure farmers of future markets and assure taxpayers that high subsidy costs will not return. To that end, he has outlined the following specific steps:

1. Commit to a program of new market development for farm commodities.

2. Expand Commodity Credit Corporation

credit by making it a revolving fund rather than a budget item.

3. Lower Commodity Credit Corporation interest rates to expand exports.

4. Extend Commodity Credit Corporation repayment period to five years (from three years).

5. Increase Title 1, Public Law 480, credit availability to $3 billion (it was previously $1.5 billion, but Carter cut it to $750 million).

6. Under Title 12 of the Agriculture Trade Expansion Act of 1978, extend Commodity Credit Corporation credit availability to individual exporters, rather than just countries (Carter has failed to implement this).

7. Expand Commodity Credit Corporation credit to poultry and red meats, thereby increasing meat/poultry exports and assisting the domestic livestock industry by expanding feed grain demand on a long-term basis.

8. Immediate implementation of U.S. Trade Mission offices approved under the Agriculture Trade Expansion Act of 1978 (20 were approved but Carter has implemented only three).

9. Title 3 calls for forgiveness of Title 1 obligations if the recipient country uses the funds for agricultural development. This forgiveness should be targeted at livestock industry expansion, thereby assuring long-term demand for feed grains.

10. Immediate action to lift the 175 percent "cap" on the call for feed grains under government loan by the Secretary of Agriculture, and extend the period from three years to five years.

11. Provide long-term, low-interest loans to farmers for further expansion of on-farm storage to handle embargoed supplies and keep supplies in private channels. ★

National Security

In a time of peace it is always difficult to define the essential defense needs of this country. With global interests and global responsibilities, the United States can never be altogether sure what threats it may have to face, when and under what circumstances. The known and continuing rivalry with the Soviet Union and the unknown and unpredictable twists and turns of Third World politics and foreign policies combine to produce a kind of tense uncertainty about the course of international affairs, even in the absence of any particular crisis. Moreover, the nature of our relationships with our Free World allies are not wholly firm in the facing of crises.

In addressing the complex sets of problems related to American national security issues, Governor Connally has been able to draw upon his experiences as Secretary of the Navy, his involvement in international monetary and trade issues as Secretary of the Treasury and his multinational associations as banker and lawyer. There is nothing about his approach to world affairs that is parochial or simplistic.

Governor Connally sees the United States locked into a long-term "struggle for nothing less than global leadership," involving competition "for the resources of the world . . . but also a struggle for the minds of men."

The first element in his program to rebuild American strength and influence is the assertion of will. He decries what he views as a kind of general defeatism that has produced a weary accommodation by the United States to one communist victory after another.

"This country," he told the Philadelphia World Affairs Council, "has got to demonstrate to other freedom-loving countries that we have the will and determination to wage psychological warfare against communist tyranny.

"We can begin by pointing out the clear fact that communism is *not* the wave of the future but a dangerous undertow which threatens to suck civilization to its doom. We must be willing to extol the virtues of freedom in a proud and positive way, because the truth is on our side."

Words are, however, not enough, and Governor Connally makes clear that the United States must have the military strength to defend its vital interests. In particular, he declares that we must not allow "control of Middle East oil by hostile forces or destruction of the oil fields during a new war in the region." He calls for immediate efforts "to establish within the Middle East region a rough balance of military power with the Soviet Union." To that end he advocates the stationing of U.S. Air Force components at the former Israeli airfields in the Sinai, if possible, and a new Fifth Fleet in the Indian Ocean able to operate in the Arabian Gulf area.

Above all, he sees American security interests in the Middle East tied to a balanced and comprehensive settlement of the Arab-Israeli conflict, not just a separate Egyptian-Israeli peace treaty. For that overall settlement to be accomplished he calls for a just and mutually acceptable live-and-let-live arrangement between Israel and a Palestinian homeland. The continuing bitter conflict Israeli-Palestinian relationships he sees as one of the most significant advantages for the Soviet Union and, thus, one of the greatest threats to American long-term interests in the region.

For the United States to continue to play its global role, Governor Connally sees it to be absolutely essential that the United States move as rapidly as possible to restore the overall "military balance of power between the United States and the Soviet Union." He says that the balance has already been tipped in the direction of the Soviet Union inasmuch as "the growth in the size and capability of Soviet strategic forces has been unprecedented for a decade and a half." The United States, he declares, cannot permit Soviet military

superiority to be established and maintained. Such a situation would destroy American influence in the world and make our own domestic economy "increasingly vulnerable."

John Connally, for all his insistence on a stepped-up military arsenal for the United States and its allies, takes the long view concerning our national security needs at the end of this century and beyond and sees our ultimate defense linked to "renewable energy sources," food and industrial raw materials. "In the late 20th century the key to national security will be *sustainability*."

In an interdependent world, in a nation that has linked its daily life to the raw materials and the product needs of other countries, national security and well-being are tied to economic and ecological conditions seemingly far removed from guns and air bases. They aren't. All the really serious problems are interrelated and must be dealt with from a position of strength and in a spirit of confidence.

We must face the fact, Governor Connally declares, that "a new diplomacy must be developed, characterized by political and commerical dynamics and, above all, realism. It is time to abandon tip-toe diplomacy and to take full advantage of all opportunities to advance national, political and economic interests abroad." ★

Acknowledgments

Shelly Katz: 68, 72, 73 bottom, 74, 78, 91 top, 95 top, 101, 104 bottom, 109 top left.

San Antonio Light: 109

San Antonio Express News: 15 left, 24 top, 25 bottom, 34, 35 bottom, 36, 37, 56, 57, 58, 59 top, 91, 110

The Curtis Publishing Company: 1, 3, 17 top bottom left, 40, 41, 44, 46,47,49, 73 top, 106

Eric David Loring: 75 top, 80, 81, 83, 85, 86 bottom, 92, 93, 94, 95 bottom, 98, 99, 100, 105, 108

John H. Jenkins collection: 26, 27, 29 top

Austin American Statesman: 29 bottom

Michael Chritton, Quad City Times: 96 top

Jim Young, Indianapolis Star: 91 bottom

Official White House Photo: introduction

United States Navy: 12, 13, 21

Ronald Anderson: 18

Craig Sikes: 86 bottom

Anna Chennault, courtesy of: 40 bottom

Chicago Photographers: 96 bottom

University of Texas Cactus: 6, 7, 8, 9

Texas State Archives: 2, 4, 5, 10, 11, 16, 20, 22, 23, 24 bottom, 32, 33, 39

R.L. Phinney: 14

Associated Press: 82

"Today Show": 86

Wendol Jarvis: 100

James E. Markam: 52, 53, 54, 55, 60, 61, 63, 64, 65, 69, 70, 71, 74, 75 bottom, 76, 77

Santa Gertrudis Journal: 48, 50, 51, 62

The Ledger Enquirer, Columbus, Ga.: 102, 103

UPI: 39

Cashen/Stout: 87

John Ebling: 100

Kay Marvin: 66